USEFUL TENANT TIPS

Ensuring Your Health, Safety, Comfort, and Security as a Renter

JIM CAMP

Tenant Tips: Ensuring Your Health, Safety, Comfort, and Security as a Renter
Published by MHI Publishing
Westminster, CO

Copyright ©2025 by Jim Camp. All rights reserved.

No part of this book may be reproduced in any form or by any mechanical means, including information storage and retrieval systems without permission in writing from the publisher/author, except by a reviewer who may quote passages in a review.

All images, logos, quotes, and trademarks included in this book are subject to use according to trademark and copyright laws of the United States of America.

Paperback ISBN: 979-8-9921790-0-2
eBook ISBN: 979-8-9921790-1-9
HOUSE & HOME / Moving & Relocation

Cover and interior design by Victoria Wolf, wolfedesignandmarketing.com; Publishing management by KLR Literary Management. Copyrights owned by Jim Camp.

This book has been Human Authored as recognized by the Authors Guild. "Human Authored" means that the text of the book was written by a human and not generated by AI.

Although the author and publisher have made every effort to ensure that the information in this book was correct at press time, the author and publisher do not assume and hereby disclaim any liability to any party for any loss, damage, or disruption caused by errors or omissions, whether such errors or omissions result from negligence, accident, or any other cause.

QUANTITY PURCHASES: Schools, companies, professional groups, clubs, and other organizations may qualify for special terms when ordering quantities of this title. For information, email jd007c@gmail.com.

All rights reserved by Jim Camp and MHI Publishing.
Printed in the United States of America.

To my late parents, whose guidance while I was growing up led me to be who I am today. For that ... *I'm forever grateful.*

"The only source of knowledge is experience."

—Albert Einstein

CONTENTS

Introduction ix

Deciding Where to Live... 1

The Walkthrough 7

Lease Agreement 15

Before You Move In... 17

Security and Crime Prevention 19

Health and Safety 27

Environmental Concerns 37

Attic Areas and Crawl Spaces 41

Conclusion 45

FAQs 47

Move-In/Out Checklist 51

Work Order Request Form 57

Personal Inventory List.. 61

Acknowledgments 67

About the Author 69

INTRODUCTION

MY NAME IS JIM CAMP, the founder and owner of Metropolitan Home Inspections in the Denver, Colorado area. I am a certified home inspector through ASHI (American Society of Home Inspectors), licensed with the State of Colorado and certified through NRPP (National Radon Proficiency Program) to conduct radon testing. I have been evaluating properties of all types and ages throughout Colorado since December 1993. My primary business is inspecting single-family residences and small commercial buildings for buyers, sellers ready to place their home on the market, those who inherit estates, or investors. However, on occasion, I will receive a request to inspect a rental property for a client, especially if it is a rent-to-own.

I was inspired to write this book after years of inspecting hundreds of rental properties for tenants that were not well maintained. In addition, I often discovered that when an investor bought a "fix-n-flip" property for use as a rental, the behind the scenes, such as attic or crawlspace areas, were untouched, and that is where I would find many issues related to health, safety, or even structural concerns. This guidebook is therefore primarily designed for properties managed by an owner who does not employ a professional management company, and in rare cases a management company that may not be as active as they should be in maintaining a rental property.

Tenants are hungry for information and guidance. Many of the tenants I have spoken with over the years have never been informed about what to do if they encounter a problem, much less the importance of accurately reporting it to a landlord (one who owns the property) or a property manager (one who manages the property for the landlord).* This book is designed to provide that guidance. The information contained here will help you live in a more comfortable, safer, and secure environment. Not all of the content will apply to every situation and all renters, especially when someone is renting a manufactured (mobile and modular) home. But experience has shown me how valuable this information can be. *You don't know what you don't know.*

Typical problems may range from structural issues and water leaks to cracked or broken windows; exterior doors or windows that will not open, close, or latch properly; loose or leaking toilets; damaged or inoperative appliances; sewer backups; pest infestation (such as rodents or insects); and marginal or inoperative heating/cooling systems. I think you get the idea.

> *A landlord may also be the property manager. It all depends on if they want to pay a fee for a third-party manager and distance themselves from the day-to-day interactions with the tenants. For simplicity, I will use the term "property manager" throughout this book.*

INTRODUCTION

Further complicating the issue is a hesitation on the part of the property manager to be proactive and attend to an issue in a timely and professional manner. Simply put, a few property managers do not view *all* issues within a rental property as a top priority. That is why it's so important to identify, document, and obtain photos of any issue you may have and submit it in writing to the property manager as soon as you discover it. This is essential, especially if it directly affects your health, safety, or security. The Work Order Report Form (at the back of this guidebook) is designed for that purpose, in case the property manager does not have such a form. Document everything and do not rely on verbal communication.

Please keep in mind that while general repairs and upgrades are the responsibility of the property manager, they may invoice a tenant or deduct all or a portion of the damage or security deposit if the tenant causes any damage to the property or performs unauthorized repairs. If you do happen to cause damage to the property, you should not make any repairs yourself, (or do a "cover-up" for your mistake), but be completely honest with the property manager about the situation. He or she should have someone they contract for maintenance or repairs, whether on staff or an outside contractor. Instead, it would be wise of you to take photos of the damage before any repairs are made and after any repairs are done, just to protect yourself.

Far too many property managers are only concerned with one thing ... *collecting the rental payment*. However, there are some responsible property managers out there, and this guidebook is not meant to label *all* property managers as uncooperative. Instead, it's designed to inform you about what you may encounter and what you can do to help protect yourself while living on someone else's property.

USEFUL TENANT TIPS

Whether you have just moved into the property or have been there for a while, you will be able to benefit from this guidebook. While some of this material may not apply or be of a concern to you at this time, it's still important to know, especially if you tend to move often. The excitement and/or anxiety of a move may cause some people to overlook many issues, whether personal, health, or environmental. This guidebook will hopefully help you understand your new home and ensure your time there is happy and safe.

DECIDING WHERE TO LIVE

ALL OF US WOULD LIKE TO LIVE in a desirable neighborhood, but given the current economic conditions and other factors, that is not always possible. Your priority should be to evaluate your situation and select an area of a city or town within your budget. Secondly, shop around. Review the places you're looking at and compare them with other similar rentals in the area. Consider whether you need a detached single-family home, a condominium, or if a town or patio home would be a better choice, especially if you want or need a garage or an extra storage area.

Decide what type of place you really need. You should not have to "settle" for just any place to live, but it is important to plan for what works best for you before you sign the lease.

You should expect to pay more or less in rent depending upon the location, type, age, or condition of the property and the amenities it has to offer. Like everything else in life, you get what you pay for, so choose wisely and don't let others pressure your decision.

After the COVID-19 pandemic, rental rates have increased along with everything else, and there may not be anything in a particular city within your budget. If this is the case, you may have to refocus your efforts and look elsewhere.

Once you have determined where you would prefer to live, you should drive around the neighborhood at different times of the day and night to observe the surroundings. This way you will have a better idea of what's going on throughout the day. This may be particularly helpful if you have an unusual schedule, sleep during the day, or if you have a business that requires you to work from home.

Next, it would benefit you to go to the website trulia.com and check out the rentals that are available, along with the schools and crime rate in the area you are interested in. Contact the local police department to enquire about the neighborhood, specifically if any drug activity or methamphetamine (meth) labs were ever discovered. This is a major concern in deciding if you want to live in that area, especially if you have children.

Once you have a concise list of places you are interested in, you should drive up to the property and note the condition of the exterior. This speaks volumes about the property manager's attitude toward the property and quite possibly the health, safety, security, and comfort of the tenants. If the place looks like a disaster zone, you should consider looking elsewhere to live. Remember to keep your eyes and ears open.

Below may be a few signs that the property manager is more interested in collecting the rent than maintaining or upgrading the property:

- Peeling paint, damaged siding, deteriorated sidewalks or parking areas, abandoned or randomly parked vehicles on a lawn or sidewalk, missing or torn screens, dead trees, or overgrown vegetation
- Personal items stored outside on the decks, walkways, or breezeways, which indicates there may not be any designated areas for a tenant to store their personal items. Furthermore, this may indicate there are no rules, regulations, or covenants, or that they are not enforced.
- Insufficient or undesignated parking areas for tenants and/or visitors
- Lack of exterior and/or security lighting
- Too much trash and not enough containers
- Unlocked or unsecured shared areas, such as utility rooms in multifamily complexes, which suggest these areas are open to anyone
- Damaged or deteriorated balconies, decks, patios, railings, fences, gates, windows, etc.

It's impossible for me to list everything I have seen, but you get the idea.

If you happen to see a neighbor out and about, you may want to stop and introduce yourself and tell them you are thinking about moving into the complex or area. You would be amazed at how much information can be obtained by asking a few simple questions. A few examples would be: How long have you lived here? What do you like about the area? Have you had any problems with the property manager, other tenants, or neighbors?

On the flip side, if the landscaping is well manicured, the parking areas, walkways, and exterior are in good condition and well illuminated, and the place looks more like a hotel, the property manager likely cares both about the property *and* the tenant. This may be the type of place you would want to call home.

YOU HAVE FINALLY FOUND THE PLACE .... WHAT NEXT?

Once you have found the place where you think you might want to live, contact the property manager or rental office and schedule to meet with them. Don't go into the meeting blindly. Below is a list of questions that will help you prepare for your visit. (Please note some of these questions may not apply, depending if you're interested in living in a multifamily complex, detached residence, or manufactured home.)

- Why did the last tenant leave?
- How often do you raise the rent?
- Will I be supplied with a list of emergency contact numbers?
- Where is the emergency evacuation plan posted?
- Are the locks changed or rekeyed after a tenant leaves, and who in your organization is authorized to have a universal key?
- What is the policy for entering into the unit when repairs are needed?
- Do you have a procedure and forms for documenting any issues I may encounter?
- How often are the electrical, plumbing, heating, and cooling systems evaluated to ensure they are safe and dependable?

- Has the property ever been tested for radon or mold?
- How often is the drain and waste piping scoped?

Assuming you feel comfortable with the answers to your questions, your next step is to arrange for a walkthrough so you can really look the place over.

THE WALKTHROUGH

THE WALKTHROUGH IS YOUR CHANCE to inspect your potential home with your own eyes. A thorough walkthrough covers a lot of details you should track (and also document). You may want to use the Move-In Checklist at the end of this guidebook, as it could be very useful. The checklist is designed so you won't miss anything of importance.

The rental you are interested in may be currently occupied. The tenant(s) may be home at the time you schedule your walkthrough and, if they are, ask the property manager if they were notified (in writing) of the date and time of the walkthrough. If the tenant was notified, you should proceed. If the property manager says "no" or hesitates for even a moment in answering your question, the tenant may not have had any knowledge of the arrangement. If this is the case, it's in your best interest to reschedule the walkthrough for another time. The last thing you want is confrontation. Besides, it's common courtesy (and is usually required in most jurisdictions or even included in the lease agreement) for the property manager to notify the current tenant when and for what purpose they want to access the property. I would argue that it's another red flag if the property manager hasn't notified the tenant, because that says something about how they might treat you, after you move in.

If you happen to conduct your walkthrough when the tenant is home, you must respect their privacy and should not be critical of how they live. *Keep the visit brief and remember at this juncture you are there to see if the place fits your needs.*

If, after the initial walkthrough, you decide that this is the place for you and all your questions have been answered to your satisfaction, inform the property manager that you are ready to proceed—but don't ever feel pressured to do so.

Once the current tenant has moved out and the property is vacant, schedule another walkthrough with the property manager, but this time bring a camera or use the camera feature on your phone. Inform the property manager that you would like to take a video of the walkthrough, so you have it for future reference. The property manager may be hesitant because everything they say will be on record, but if they are honest in all they are telling you, they should not have an issue. If the property manager says no, ask them why and document what they say.

As you walk through the property, point out anything unusual, such as strange odors, stains, missing electrical cover plates, damaged or dirty appliances, flooring, walls, ceilings, and so on. Operate *all* the plumbing fixtures, lights, windows, and doors and document any dirty, defective, or missing items. You will want to have these cleaned, repaired, or replaced (respectively) *before* you move in. Also, have the property manager demonstrate the operation of the heating and cooling systems, and show you where all the shutoffs (electrical, heating, water heater, main water for the plumbing, and so on) are located, and how to operate them. This will be very helpful if there is ever an emergency.

You may want to inquire whether the rental has been vacant for more than a couple of months, as this may be a sign that something might be wrong with the rental, the property manager, or both. However, before jumping to any conclusions, you could consult with the property manager about the vacancy rate in the complex as a whole, as some areas of town may have a higher vacancy rate than others. Document whatever the property manager tells you. If the place you are interested in has a high vacancy rate, or lower rental rates than other comparable places, there must be a reason, and I usually suggest you move on.

If you feel uncomfortable inspecting the rental yourself, you could hire the services of a qualified home inspector. After all, it's really no different than if you were looking to buy a house. This way, you will have a professional and unbiased report of the property. In addition, home inspectors are trained to look for anything that may affect your health, safety, or security. Isn't a few hundred dollars worth your peace of mind?

Inform the property manager of your intentions, as they may be reluctant to have a third party roam through the property without their knowledge.

WHAT TO FOCUS ON
The following list may seem unnecessary, but it can be extremely useful as you conduct your walkthrough. If nothing else, it should keep you focused on why you are there.

Lighting
Check to see if all the lights work. If not, the bulbs should be replaced, and the operation of the fixture verified.

Switches
Any damaged switches or missing knobs should be replaced. If you find a dimmer switch on a fluorescent light or outlet, request that it be replaced as this type of switch is not compatible with these devices and could be a safety hazard.

Electrical Receptacles
All receptacles must be protected with a proper cover plate and none of them should exhibit damage or charring.

Ground Fault Circuit Interrupter (GFCI) Protection
Ask or check to see if any ground fault protection is installed. This may take the form of a special breaker in the electrical panel, or a special receptacle (equipped with "test" and "reset" buttons). Depending on the age of the property, these devices may not be installed. If they are, familiarize yourself with where they are located and how to reset them. You may sometimes find a dwelling with only a single GFCI receptacle, usually in a bathroom (or even in the garage), but ideally, this important protection should also be present in the other bathrooms, kitchen, laundry, garage, and the exterior as well (depending upon the age and type of dwelling).

Exterior
Verify each entry door is in good condition and opens, closes, latches, and locks properly. If applicable, check the condition of the garage door, windows, floor, ceiling, and so on.

Check the overall condition of the site, which includes walkways, driveways, porches, patios, balconies, fencing, parking areas, swimming pools, or other features unique to the property.

Roof

Regardless of the type of rental you're considering, the roof is off-limits. However, you could be inquisitive regarding the age and overall condition of the roof for your own information.

If you experience water leaks once you move in, during or even after a rain or snow storm, contact the property manager immediately.

Windows

Verify each window opens, closes, and latches properly. Check for failed thermopanes (double- or triple-insulated glass with moisture or condensation between the panes), cracked or broken glass, and water stains around the sill. If the glass is cracked or broken, request to have it replaced. Property managers may choose not to replace any failed thermopanes, so be sure to document which ones are affected. The document may encourage them to replace it or protect you if they don't.

Surfaces

Look for anything unusual on the ceilings, walls, and floors, including a freshly painted area that might be hiding a previous water leak or recent repair. Take pictures, document what you see, and ask questions if you notice anything unusual.

Appliances

Operate all the appliances and make sure they have been cleaned and are in good working order. In some cases, you may be required to have your own appliances, so make sure they will fit in the space allotted.

Cabinets & Countertops

Look into all the cabinets and check the operation of the doors, drawers, and condition of the countertops to be sure they have been cleaned and are odor free. If they are stained or show signs of repair, document it and take a photograph.

Heating & Cooling Systems

The property manager should explain what type of system is installed and demonstrate the operation of the heating and cooling systems, along with the location of the emergency shutoffs for each. The only maintenance you should be responsible for is to possibly change the filter (in a gas or electric forced air furnace) and to keep the area around these appliances free and clear of any debris or personally stored items. Ask the property manager how often these appliances are serviced.

Hot Water

The property manager should explain what type of equipment produces hot water in the rental, and the do's and don'ts of each. This could be a gas or electric tank water heater, tankless or on-demand heater, boiler, or a community system, such as in an apartment building. If you have issues with the hot water later, contact the property manager.

Smoke and Carbon Monoxide Detectors

Look around to see if any smoke and carbon monoxide detectors, fire extinguishers, or even sprinkler systems (if applicable) are installed. If not, you are encouraged to contact the local jurisdiction's building code enforcement department to find out what the minimum safety requirements are for rental properties. At the very least, smoke detectors should be installed and placed in areas where they are currently required. *Carbon monoxide detectors are required to be within fifteen feet of all bedrooms (at least here in Denver and surrounding areas), with at least one on every floor.* For added protection, renters may purchase plug-in detectors, which are portable and easy to install.

YOU MUST INSIST that the rental is a clean and safe environment for you and your family. Let's face it, you don't know who the previous tenant(s) were and the living standards they had or didn't have. You can usually tell if the property manager hired a professional cleaning service or had someone come in and just give the place the once-over to save a few dollars. This is particularly true with painting. If you see that some or all of the switches, hinges, or anything else that doesn't move have been painted, you know right away the property manager doesn't care much about the quality of the work done around the property.

LEASE AGREEMENT

SINCE THE LEASE AGREEMENT is a legal document, have it reviewed by a real estate attorney, especially if the property manager is the owner and not affiliated with a professional rental agency. Furthermore, do not rely on verbal communication, as everything pertinent to you renting a place should be in writing. For example, if the owner states that he/she has plans for a remodel, replacing an appliance, or upgrading the electrical or plumbing, have them put it in writing with dates, including detailed information on the work to be done. Request a copy of the document and keep it with your records.

> *Trick of the trade: Once you are satisfied with the contents of the agreement, make an inconspicuous mark on the document. For example, you may want to place a mark of some sort at the bottom left corner or completely fill in an "o" or "0". You should do this before you meet and sign it in front of the property manager. The reason for the mark*

is simple. Occasionally, a property manager may give you one document to review, but have you sign another document that looks like the original but has subtle changes in the wording.

For example, these changes may include the length of the lease, monthly payments, or the amount of a damage/security deposit. The mark will ensure that you are signing the document you and/or your attorney actually read.

The property manager will obtain a credit report and other personal information such as work history, background check, motor vehicle record, and/or character references. *Reaffirm that the information they obtain is true, but not for public knowledge.*

BEFORE YOU MOVE IN

LOCKS AND SECURITY SYSTEM

For your protection, safety, and security, request that all the exterior locks (to the rental itself and any storage lockers or interior/exterior closets associated with the rental) be rekeyed or replaced. You simply don't know how many keys were made or who has them, especially if the rental has had many tenants (or even property managers) in the past. You will most definitely run into some resistance here, but state your case and tell them that if anything happens while you are there, and someone enters the home (without an obvious break-in), you are holding them responsible. That should get their attention. Hopefully, they will want to work with you, but if rekeying is not their policy, there are other precautions you may want to take to increase your protection. Check with a home security company, and/or a home improvement center for what products would best suit your needs. The goal is to protect yourself.

Before you decide to install some type of security system, inform the property manager of your intentions, as this may be in violation of your lease agreement. Remember, you are responsible for any damage to the walls, doors, windows, and so on caused by the installation—especially if these items are installed without the property manager's knowledge or approval.

DOCUMENT!

Be sure to take digital photos or videos of the interior, and any major components such as the water heater, furnace, and appliances, as well as any damage you find. This way you will have documentation on the condition of the property before you move in. These records may come in very handy if you run into problems in trying to recoup your damage or security deposit when you move out.

> *To further protect yourself, give a copy of these photos or videos to the property manager with a note (dated and signed) indicating that this is the condition of the property when you moved in and that this is their copy to file. Have the property manager either sign for the copy or acknowledge via email that he or she received it.*

Occasionally, the property manager may accuse a tenant of damaging, altering, or removing something from the property. The photos or videos you have will protect you from having to pay for something you didn't do.

SECURITY AND CRIME PREVENTION

ONCE YOU DECIDE TO MOVE INTO THE PROPERTY, you may want to obtain all the names and numbers, and possibly even photos, of all the employees you will be in contact with while you are staying on the property. This way, if someone contacts you for repairs, or asks for additional personal information, or anything else out of the ordinary, you can check them against the list. You should report anyone not on the list to the property manager and/or authorities, if needed.

If the rental is an apartment or condominium, ask what kind of security is provided for the tenants. These systems may include built-in security cameras, roving patrols, and locks or key fobs for common areas. The less security provided by the property manager, the more security you will need to arrange for yourself.

Mobile home parks typically have little or no security. If the rental is a single-family dwelling, a unit within a multifamily complex, or a townhouse or patio home, there will probably be little or no security either, unless it happens to be in a gated community or the home is equipped with a security system.

INVENTORY LIST

It is highly recommended that you keep an inventory list with any applicable serial and model numbers and current photos (preferably digital) of everything you own. A list is especially useful for items that don't have such numbers or are too small to physically mark, such as jewelry, watches, rings, necklaces, pendants, bracelets, and the like. You may want to contact your insurance company for an inventory booklet. If they do not have any booklets, you could use the inventory list that is included within this book.

You may think that filling out an inventory list is a waste of time, but if you have ever had anything stolen or lost in a fire, you would quickly understand the importance of going through this exercise. A photo and a description would prove that you owned a particular item, and it would be extremely helpful should you ever file a claim with your insurance company or report the loss to the police department. In addition, the more information you have about your belongings, the better your chances are of having them returned, especially if someone tries to pawn them or sell them at a flea market. You may want to consider marking anything of value with a unique identifier (but *not* with your social security number, license plate number, or any other personal information), so that they can be easily identified if stolen and/or resold.

Once your inventory list is complete, make a copy, and file the original separately in a safe place and/or save it on a memory stick or Dropbox or Google Drive. You could also send a copy to your insurance agent, a family member, or a good friend. It's important to keep the list up to date as you obtain more and more "stuff." And if you ever sell or just get rid of an item, delete it from the list.

VARY YOUR ROUTINES

Another hint to keep yourself and your belongings safer is to become "unpredictable." We are creatures of habit and tend to get into a groove and stay there. We always seem to park in the same area at a shopping mall, sit in the same area at a theater, or drive the same way to work. It is in your best interest to alter your routine occasionally. For instance, install timers for lights, and alter the time you get up in the morning, leave for the day, return home from work, or take the dog for a walk. When you drive to or from work, try taking a different route and see if anyone is following you. *Always be aware of your surroundings.*

PERSONAL SAFETY

To reduce the chances of having your car broken into, have *nothing* visible. If you must keep items in your car, hide them under a seat or in the trunk, but *never* keep anything of value and in plain sight inside of the car. These items would include a cell phone, briefcase, mail, books, magazines, or anything else that may have your name and address on it or be of some value. You may want to consider installing an alarm system and registering the car in a national database, where an ID number is etched on the windows. You may also want to check with your insurance company to determine the frequency at which the type of car you are driving is broken into or stolen. This can be a revelation and cause you to take additional measures.

Once again, you should always be aware of your surroundings, regardless of whether you're at home, work, shopping, at a restaurant, or even stopped in traffic. It may be wise to purchase pepper spray, a whistle, a horn, or some audible device to warn others that you may be in trouble. In addition, you should always let others know where you are going and about what time you plan on returning. It also may be a good idea to let your friends and colleagues know what type of car you drive and the license number as well.

If your rental is in a multifamily complex, you may want to find out if there's assigned parking, but also proper lighting not only in the parking and walkway areas but also around the building, especially at the entrances and corners.

Rentals with parking garages will most likely be secure, but even then, make sure no one follows you into the garage while driving in and try to back into your space if you can. This way when you leave your car you can look around to see if anyone is just sitting in another car waiting, loitering, or appearing to approach you.

If the rental is a single-family dwelling or duplex, make sure that the exterior lighting works and is on. If you suspect someone is following you on your way home, drive past where you live and go around the block a couple of times to see if they follow you. If this is the case, you could drive to the nearest convenience or grocery store where there are many people or even a police station if one is nearby.

IMPORTANT SUGGESTION

Due to the ever-increasing problem of identity theft, I do not advise you to use your SSN or anything else that may identify who you are to mark your belongings. Our reasoning behind this is simple: if an item is stolen, the thief may not be aware that it is marked, or equipped with a location tag, as they are only interested in getting in and out as quickly as possible. If they later discover information that can lead to your identity, the stage is set for you to go on the defensive (and you do not want to do this).

Our suggestion would be to create a unique identifier that does not include identifying details such as your name, SSN, or address. You may also opt to purchase a smart tag and app for the more expensive items. For example, let's say that you are an avid skier. You could use a phrase like "snowboard" or "chairlift" to mark your personal items. Look at it this way: the item or items may have been stolen, but in this case, your personal identity has not been compromised.

RENTER'S INSURANCE

If you do not have renter's insurance, I strongly recommend you obtain a policy. It's not that expensive and it's for your own protection, even if you don't think you have that much to insure. A policy could range anywhere from ten to thirty-five dollars per month, or more depending upon the area of the country. If you are in doubt, contact your insurance agent for guidance on what type of insurance would best suit your needs. You should also mark or identify all your personal belongings of value, such as stereo equipment, cell phones, personal storage devices, game consoles, TV sets, pictures, paintings, or anything else that can be stolen and sold for quick cash. Marks can include a stamp, etching, paint, or barcode.

USEFUL TENANT TIPS

The chart below has additional suggestions or actions that may also be taken to protect yourself. While many of these actions are meant for homeowners, some may also be utilized by you, the tenant, or even possibly submitted to the owner for consideration.

ADDITIONAL SECURITY MEASURES

Doors	Exterior
Install a 180-degree peephole.	Install motion detection fixtures.
Ensure locks are at least 40 inches from any window.	Trim trees "up" to 6' and shrubs "down" to 3' or less.
Install solid core doors w/o any windows or sidelights.	Ensure house numbers are clearly visible from street.
Ensure door and frame have tight fit.	Ensure all entry doors are well lit.
Install dead bolt lock with full travel.	Ensure all sides of house visible to neighbors.
Rekey or replace locks.	Remove any abandoned vehicles, trash, etc.
Do not install any pet doors within a door or exterior wall.	

SECURITY AND CRIME PREVENTION

Windows	Garage
Verify that all windows lock. Install auxiliary locks on metal windows. Verify that the window can be secured in place when opened. Use curtains to cover all of the window. Verify that window air conditioners are secured from the inside. Keep windows locked or blocked at all times. Secure basement windows.	Ensure the garage door opens and closes properly. Verify the windows/doors are in good condition. Cover or install security film over any windows. Keep garage door closed at all times when not in use. Ensure all the lights work.
Vacation Tips	**Additional Tips**
Notify a trusted neighbor that you are leaving. Give your trusted neighbor your itinerary/phone number. Stop newspapers. Stop mail and package delivery. Install timers to lights. Have a trusted neighbor check the exterior often. Have exterior cared for (lawn, snow removal, etc.).	Don't boast about what you own. Store all weapons in a secure place. Keep serial numbers of all high-dollar items. Keep bills, statements, jewelry, cash, etc. out of sight. Keep anything of value away from the windows. Change your routine often. Get to know your neighbors.

HEALTH AND SAFETY

IN ADDITION TO SECURITY and crime prevention, a healthy and safe environment should be another priority.

Carbon Monoxide Detectors

As stated earlier, carbon monoxide detectors are strongly recommended. Chances are there will not be any in the rental, so you must install them. Regardless of which type or brand you buy, follow the installation instructions to the letter.

Demonstrations

The property manager should demonstrate the operation of all the appliances and other equipment that may be associated with the property. This includes the stove, oven, dishwasher, microwave, trash compactor, disposal, ice maker, cooktop, kitchen exhaust system, water softener, garage door opener, and electric gates. This demonstration will also give you a chance to make sure the appliances work. Though you may have reviewed the function of appliances during a walkthrough, it is important to check again as you move in.

Emergency Call List
Request to have a list of all the emergency contact names and phone numbers that you may need. This list should include the fire and police departments, the property manager and all approved contractors, as well as the procedure for after business hours, in case of an emergency.

Emergency Escape Plan
Request to see the emergency escape plan, *especially* if it is a multi-family complex. This plan should be reviewed to see if it is current and effective. If there isn't an escape plan, devise one of your own and stress the importance of this plan to every member of your family. If you are located on the first or second floor, an escape ladder (designed for this type of application) may be appropriate and encouraged. Store this ladder near a window so it can be accessed quickly in case of an emergency. If the rental is in a high-rise, there should be an evacuation plan posted on each floor.

If there are security or burglar bars installed over low-level windows, be sure they can be opened from the inside. If they are fixed and cannot be opened, report this to the property manager and insist they be removed or replaced. These bars may deter intruders but will also prevent you from making a quick exit if a fire or some other type of emergency blocked the other points of exit.

Emergency Lighting
You may want to purchase one or more dependable flashlights (rechargeable, battery, or induction) for emergencies.

HEALTH AND SAFETY

Exterior Lighting
Look around to see if there is adequate lighting on the exterior to safely illuminate all walkways, entryways, parking, and common areas. Check to see if there are any obvious trip hazards.

Operating Manuals
Request operating manuals for all the appliances, including smoke and/or carbon monoxide detectors, security systems, timers, garage door openers, sprinkler systems, or whatever applies. If there are no manuals, ask the property manager to purchase them, or try downloading them from the manufacturers' websites.

Smoke Detectors
Check to see if smoke detectors are installed and verify the operation of each with the test button. If none are present, you should ask the property manager to purchase and install at least one for each bedroom and one on every floor. If the rental already has these installed, test them to see if they operate. If not, a new battery should be installed and tested again. If the device still does not respond, have the property manager replace it.

In homes built in 1989 and after, the detectors are required to be "hardwired," or interconnected into the electrical system of the home, which means if one detector sounds off, the others would respond as well. There should be a red or green LED to indicate power is supplied to the device. If you do not see this light, ask to have the system checked out. Bear in mind that you can also test hardwired systems by pressing the test button, as they all should have a battery backup.

A fire-suppression or sprinkler system may be installed inside the rental, especially if it is within a multifamily complex or a home in a remote area away from any fire department. Learn the details of this system from the property manager, but *never* tamper with any components of this system.

FIREPLACES, WOOD-BURNING STOVES, AND FIREPLACE INSERTS
Gas Fireplaces and Gas Log Sets

Gas fireplaces come in many different styles and configurations. It's very important that the property manager demonstrates the use of this appliance along with pointing out the location of the local gas shutoff valve.

Remember: If you smell gas, LEAVE THE BUILDING and call 911 once you are safely outside. Call the property manager and inform them of the situation. Do not reenter the building until you are told to do so by the local authority.

If the appliance exhibits any of the following, it should be evaluated by a gas fireplace specialist and not used until it has been certified to be safe:

- Characteristics of the flames abruptly change
- Pulsating or irregular flame
- Delayed or no ignition
- Scratched or cracked glass

Gas Fireplace Precautions and Recommendations:

- Install one or more carbon monoxide detectors.
- Do not leave any operating fireplace unattended.
- Do not touch the glass or screen (if so equipped).
- Do not burn wood or anything else in a gas fireplace.

HEALTH AND SAFETY

- Follow the manufacturer's recommendation when cleaning the glass.
- Turn the appliance off when leaving the premises or retiring for the evening.
- Keep children and pets away from the appliance at all times.
- Turn the gas supply off when leaving for extended periods of time and keep the key for the gas shutoff valve out of the reach of children.
- Do not make any adjustments to the flames or alter the pattern of the logs.
- If a wood-burning fireplace has been converted to a gas log set, make sure the damper is either removed or locked in the "fully opened" position.

Gas fireplaces are decorative appliances only, and they should never be used as a secondary heat source. They cannot be converted to burn wood or any other type of fuel, and no attempt should be made to burn wood in any gas fireplace. They cannot be altered or modified in any way, and they should always be turned off when no one is in the room or at bedtime.

PLEASE NOTE: If the rental is equipped with a ventless fireplace, you should **never** use it. A ventless fireplace is a decorative gas appliance that vents directly into the room, **not** to the exterior. If you are unsure of the type of gas fireplace installed in the rental, ask the property manager. If they don't know, contact a qualified fireplace technician.

Wood-Burning Fireplaces

The major components of a wood-burning fireplace are the mantel, hearth, firebox (lined with bricks and mortar, metal, or special removable panels), flue, and damper. You should ask the property manager when the fireplace and flue were last cleaned and certified. Keep in mind that fireplaces in rental properties are often neglected and/or misused.

If the fireplace exhibits any of the following, it should be evaluated by a fireplace specialist and not used until it has been certified to be safe:

- Charring around the opening
- Cracked firebricks along with deteriorated mortar, missing or damaged fireproof panels, or extremely warped or cracked metal walls
- Discolored or cracked glass (if so equipped)
- Inoperative or damaged screens
- Damaged or inoperative damper
- Damaged spark arrestor/rain cap on top of the flue
- Excessive buildup of soot and/or creosote inside the firebox and flue
- Dirty cleanout (if so equipped)

Wood-Burning Fireplace Precautions and Recommendations:

- Do not use any accelerants, items drenched in accelerants, or torches to get a fire started.
- Do not burn anything other than wood or manufactured logs that are approved for residential fireplaces.

- Keep all children and pets away from the fireplace at all times.
- Never leave the fireplace unattended while a fire is burning.
- Open a window for proper ventilation.
- Use of a protective screen or glass doors is highly recommended.
- Do not store anything inside of the firebox when not in use.
- Clean the firebox after every use and discard the ashes in a proper container *only when they have cooled.*
- Do not use a fireplace as a secondary heat source.

Caution: *If the firebox of the fireplace is at floor level and it is very shallow, do not use it until it has been certified by a licensed fireplace specialist.*

Wood-Burning or Pellet Stoves and Fireplace Inserts

Popular in the colder regions and mountain areas, these appliances are often used as primary or secondary heat sources. Unfortunately, they are just as often neglected, seldom cleaned, and often abused.

These stoves are constructed of heavy gauge metal. Besides the burning area, flue, and adjustable air vents, they could have any of the following features: thermostat, circulating fan, shelf or flat surface for heating, adjustable or thermostatic vent damper, heat recovery unit, door glass, and temperature gauge.

If the appliance exhibits any of the following, it should be evaluated by a qualified specialist and not used until it has been certified to be safe:

- Hot spots or discoloration of the exterior paint or finish
- Damaged or missing fireproof panels
- Missing, broken, or cracked firebricks, or cracked or excessively warped metal firebox
- Discolored or cracked door glass
- Inoperative damper
- Damaged spark arrestor/rain cap on top of the flue
- Excessive buildup of soot and/or creosote inside the firebox and flue
- Dirty cleanout (if so equipped)
- Open, loose, or disconnected joints in the flue
- Flat or negative slope in the flue
- Inadequate air supply for combustion
- Improper support for the stove
- Physical damage anywhere on the stove or flue

Stove or Insert Precautions and Recommendations:

- Never clean the outer surfaces with abrasive cleaners or sponges, as these will damage the paint.
- Do not heat any flammable liquids on the heating surface or inside the firebox.
- Do not use any accelerants, items drenched in accelerants, or torches to get a fire started.
- Do not burn anything other than wood or manufactured logs that are approved for use.
- Keep children and pets away from the stove at all times.
- Never leave the stove/insert unattended while in use.
- Open a window for proper ventilation.

HEALTH AND SAFETY

- Do not leave the door to the firebox open during operation.
- Do not store anything inside of the firebox when not in use.
- Clean the firebox after every use and discard the ashes in a proper container *only when they have cooled*.
- Never burn anything other than approved pellets in a pellet stove.

ENVIRONMENTAL CONCERNS

YOU SHOULD ALSO BE AWARE of different environmental hazards that may exist in or around your rental property. Depending upon the area, you may want to research the history or "past life" of the building site to determine its prior usage. This may be a little extreme, but it can be very interesting.

PROPERTY HISTORY

Past life	Considerations or Possible Issues
Abandoned Mines	Sinkholes or cave-ins
Burial site	Decomposed bodies
Dump site	Unstable soil, methane, other toxic gases
Gas station	Abandoned underground storage tanks, contaminated soil from oil, gas leaks, antifreeze, lubricants, etc.
Landfill	Buried equipment, trash, building materials, methane gas
Manufacturing facility	Solvents, chemicals, buried machinery, broken glass
Restaurant	Grease, solvents
Superfund site	Solvents, chemicals, toxic waste
Swamp	High water table, unsafe water, unstable soils, mosquitoes

Abandoned Fuel Tanks

There could be abandoned fuel oil or gas tanks on the property. The concern here is that these tanks may have leaked in the past and contaminated the soil, or they were removed without the proper clean-up, backfill, and soil compaction, which may result in a sinkhole.

Abandoned Mines or Landfills

Abandoned mines or landfills on or near the property can be dangerous, as they may only be covered with a few feet of soil, concrete, timbers, old cars, or plywood.

ENVIRONMENTAL CONCERNS

In a few areas, mobile home parks have been placed over landfills because the soil in these areas is too unstable to build a permanent structure. If you are renting a mobile home, you may want to check this out.

Asbestos

Asbestos was used primarily for floor tiles and exterior shingles, insulating the exhaust and supply ducts for gas heating systems, acoustic spray for textured ceilings, and as a fire retardant. If the dwelling was built before 1978 and even today, there may be a chance that this substance is present. Contrary to popular belief, asbestos is legal today. It was only illegal for two years (1989 to 1991). You may want to consult with the property manager if any testing was performed, especially if you are moving into an older building.

Chemicals and Solvents

Chemicals and/or solvents may have been used in or around the building. All chemicals and solvents should be properly labeled and stored in an approved area or locker out of the reach of small children and pets.

Lead-Based Paint

If the dwelling was constructed before 1978, there is a very good chance that lead-based paint was used. If these surfaces are in good condition, it probably won't be an issue ... but you should still be cautious. However, if the paint exhibits any flaking, blistering, cracking, or peeling, action *must* be taken, especially if there are small children.

"Lead-safe" means that the dwelling has lead paint, but it is *in good condition*. "Lead-free" means that the dwelling has no lead paint. Either way, the property manager should disclose this information.

Lead Water Supply Piping

Lead piping was used in the past for the water supply piping in older homes. If the rental house was built in the early 1920s, this piping may still exist.

Mold/Mildew

Look for any unusual staining or marks on the walls, ceilings, windows, and cabinets in the kitchen, laundry, and bathroom areas. If there is a musty or stale odor in any of the rooms or areas, this may indicate a moisture problem. If you suspect that mold or mildew is present, bring it to the attention of the property manager for further evaluation and remediation. The more you know about this health issue, the better off you are.

Radon

One of the decay products of uranium is radon gas, which is colorless, odorless, and tasteless. The chances are very slim that your property manager had the property tested, but you may want to inquire anyway. There is probably not much you can do if the rental is in a multifamily complex, but in a single-family home, duplex, or townhome you may ask the property manager if they are willing to perform a radon test. Whatever the outcome, document it.

Utilities

It's very important to know what types of utilities are supplied to the dwelling.

If the rental is an apartment or condominium, there may not be any accessible shutoffs within the unit. These may include but are not limited to water, gas, and electric. Ask the property manager for a written procedure for what you should do in case of an emergency.

ATTIC AREAS AND CRAWL SPACES

ATTICS

Attic areas contain the roof structure, insulation, wiring, exhaust ducts, and plumbing vents. However, they may also be home to rodents, insects, and water leaks. This area should be inspected during the walkthrough, because any of these conditions could mean problems for you.

Extreme temperatures in attic spaces may cause flash fires if the conditions are just right. Therefore, these areas should *never* be used for storage of personal items. Check to see that the attic is free and clear of all belongings.

One other item of concern would be if an attic in a multifamily complex is in common with an adjacent unit—it may be possible to access these other units from the attic. If so, the hatch covers should be locked down.

CRAWL SPACES

The rental may have a full or partial crawl space (an unlivable area or space beneath the main floor). These spaces are usually not very deep and are mainly used for accessing the utilities. Typically, the water shutoff valve, water supply piping, cleanouts for the sewer system, subsurface water management system (drain line with a sump pump), shutoff valve for the water supply to a sprinkler system, dryer exhaust, furnaces, and heating ducts and/or gas lines will be found in this area.

Mobile homes are unique as they are located over a pad or partial pad and supported by columns or adjustable jacks. While they also have a crawl space under the home, it's usually *at* ground level. Since the furnace and water heater are contained within the home, the major items in mobile home crawl spaces will be the utility hookups, drain and waste piping, support system, tie downs or anchoring system, and skirting.

Wherever you live, you will want to check with the property manager to find out what condition the crawl space is in. Unless you have an agreement to change the furnace filter once a month—and the furnace happens to be in the crawl space—there likely will be little reason for you to access this area in a rental.

It is important to know, however, that crawl spaces can and do harbor many environmental hazards. You will definitely want to know what condition yours is in before you move in, and even after you have been living there a while. Let's face it, no one really likes or even wants to enter these out-of-the-way places, which is why it's so important to have a well illuminated, safe, and clean environment if you have to, especially when a furnace and the main water shutoff valve may be located in this area.

POSSIBLE ATTIC AND CRAWL SPACE HEALTH AND SAFETY CONCERNS

Condition	Concern	Environmental Hazard
Animals	Health	Rabies
Debris and stored personal items	Health and Safety	Broken glass, sharp metal, nails, screws, rodents, mold and/or mildew, hidden foundation problems
Disconnected or leaking sewer lines	Health	Raw sewage is very nasty … you get the idea
Leaks from water supply lines	Health	Possible mold and/or mildew from the pooling of water
Improperly configured or disconnected furnace or water heater exhaust vent	Health	Carbon monoxide poisoning
Moisture	Health	Mold and/or mildew, termites, or carpenter ants
Rodent, insect, or reptile activity	Health	Diseases from rodents (such as hantavirus), bee or wasp activity, mosquitoes, spiders (black widows, brown recluses), snakes

CONCLUSION

I HOPE YOU FOUND THIS GUIDEBOOK insightful and useful in your search for a place to live. Since my concern is your well-being, I felt it was necessary to publish a document that gets to the core of the issues many tenants face when renting. There may be other issues that I have not mentioned, but the information within this book is what I have experienced during my career as a home inspector. Even though some of the information within this guidebook may or may not apply to your current situation, I felt it should be mentioned, as it could directly affect the health, safety, and security of you and your family in the future.

Homeownership is a wonderful thing, but I realize that circumstances do not always permit this. I wish you the best of luck wherever you call home.

If you would like information on the importance of a property inspection, please visit my website at metrohomeinspects.com.

Jim Camp
Jim Camp
Metropolitan Home Inspections
Westminster, CO

FAQS

Q. Why do I need renter's insurance?
A. While the property manager must carry distinct types of insurance on the building, their insurance does not cover your belongings, such as in cases of fire, theft, or flood. Renter's insurance is strongly recommended. It's inexpensive and may cover the contents inside of your car as well. Contact your insurance agent for more information.

Q. I don't own the place ... why should I be concerned about its condition?
A. Ensuring your and your family's health, safety, and security should be a top priority. If the building has not been maintained, that's a red flag that your health, safety, or security may be at risk. If you see that the building or grounds are in disrepair or neglected, this will almost assure you that the other systems or subsystems (electrical wiring, plumbing, heating/cooling, and so on) may be just as bad or possibly in worse condition. Visible neglect also shows that the rent collected from tenants is not applied for any repairs or upgrades to the building or for the safety, security, and comfort of the occupants.

Q. Why should I be concerned about the age of the property?

A. Older structures may not be updated with all the safety features that may be required. For instance, rental units within an older multifamily complex may not have a fire alarm or sprinkler system; properly identified emergency exits; evacuation plans or fire extinguishers; Ground Fault Circuit Interrupter or Arc Fault Circuit Interrupter protection; smoke and carbon monoxide detectors; and/or an adequate electrical service. Windows on a second story and above may not have stops to prevent them from opening too far, and decks or balconies may not have sturdy and/or enclosed railings. In addition, the rental may not conform to the Americans with Disabilities Act (ADA) for handicapped access.

Q. What if I follow your advice and still have problems with the property manager?

A. If you are having problems getting the property manager to cooperate or work with you to resolve any legitimate issues, contact a real estate attorney immediately. Make sure you have as much documentation as possible to prove there has been no cooperation with the property manager.

Q. What kinds of environmental issues might I encounter?

A. You may want to research the history of the property. After all, there may be a radon issue, the property may have been a past dump, Superfund site, or even a gas station with leaking underground storage tanks.

MOVE-IN/OUT CHECKLIST

THIS CHECKLIST IS DESIGNED for either moving into or out of a rental property.

A downloadable version is available at metrohomeinspects.com.

USEFUL TENANT TIPS

Date: _____

Address: _____

Unit #: _____

City/Zip Code: _____

Property Manager Contact: _____

Phone #: _____

PROPERTY INFORMATION:

Write down what you see and take photos. Fill in only those areas that apply or write N/A for comments if the item is not applicable to you.

MOVE-IN/OUT CHECKLIST

Exterior			
	Acceptable	Not Acceptable	Comments
Balconies:			
Decks:			
Downspouts:			
Doors:			
Driveway(s):			
Fencing:			
Gates:			
Gutters:			
Lighting:			
Parking Areas:			
Patios:			
Sidewalk(s):			
Siding:			
Windows:			
Yard:			

USEFUL TENANT TIPS

Garage: (if applicable)			
	Acceptable	Not Acceptable	Comments
Doors:			
Floor:			
Lights:			
Opener(s):			
Outlets:			
Roof:			
Walls:			
Window(s):			

MOVE-IN/OUT CHECKLIST

Interior			
Bathroom(s)	Acceptable	Not Acceptable	Comments
Doors:			
Flooring:			
Lights/Fan:			
Mirrors:			
Outlets:			
Sink(s):			
Toilet(s):			
Tub/Shower(s):			
Vanities:			
Ventilation:			
Walls/Ceiling:			
Windows:			

USEFUL TENANT TIPS

Bedroom(s)	Acceptable	Not Acceptable	Comments
Closets:			
Doors:			
Fireplaces:			
Flooring:			
Lights/Outlets:			
Vent Fan(s):			
Walls/Ceiling:			
Windows:			
Living room	Acceptable	Not Acceptable	Comments
Doors:			
Fireplaces:			
Flooring:			
Lights/Fan(s):			
Outlets:			
Walls/Ceiling:			
Windows:			

MOVE-IN/OUT CHECKLIST

Kitchen	Acceptable	Not Acceptable	Comments
Cabinets:			
Countertops:			
Doors:			
Outlets:			
Flooring:			
Lights/Fan(s):			
Microwave:			
Refrigerator:			
Sink(s):			
Stove/Oven:			
Trash Compactor/ Disposal:			
Ventilation:			
Walls/Ceiling:			
Windows:			

Other rooms	Acceptable	Not Acceptable	Comments
Doors:			
Outlets:			
Flooring:			
Lights/Fan(s):			
Walls/Ceiling:			
Windows:			

WORK ORDER REQUEST FORM

THIS FORM MAY BE COPIED or printed as many times as needed, but it is designed to report one issue at a time.

A downloadable version is available at metrohomeinspects.com.

USEFUL TENANT TIPS

Number: _____

Date Submitted: _____ Submitted To: _____

From: _____ Phone: _____

Address: _____

Unit: _____

Date Issue Discovered: _____

Description of Issue:

_____

_____

_____

_____

_____

_____

_____

_____

_____

_____

_____

_____

_____

_____

WORK ORDER REQUEST FORM

_____
_____
_____
_____
_____
_____
_____
_____
_____
_____
_____
_____
_____
_____
_____
_____
_____
_____
_____
_____

Respectfully Submitted By:

PERSONAL INVENTORY LIST

THIS LIST IS DESIGNED FOR YOU to catalog your valuables. For example, you would want to list jewelry, entertainment equipment, household appliances, pictures, paintings, furniture, clothing, computers, printers, monitors, collectibles, books, tools, power equipment, weapons, and so on. In addition, you may want to take photos or videos to show proof of ownership. All of this can be stored on Dropbox or Google Drive. The key benefit of taking a video is that you can narrate and explain each item as you progress.

This inventory may or may not be exhaustive, but at least it's a place to start. Think of it this way: it will allow you to dispose of those items you never use or even remember you had. Anything you manage to part with could be donated to the less fortunate or recycled. (Think green!)

Sure, it may seem mundane to go through this exercise, but you never know when you may need it.

Appliances

Item Description (including model and serial numbers)	Approximate Value

Bedding

Item Description	Approximate Value

Bicycles

Item Description (trikes, skateboards, scooters, etc.)	Approximate Value

PERSONAL INVENTORY LIST

Clothing	
Item Description (shirts, shoes, dresses, coats)	Approximate Value

Electronics	
Item Description (including m/n and s/n for computers, printers, monitors, phones, tablets, and other devices)	Approximate Value

Collectibles	
Item Description (paintings, photographs, comic books, antiques, artifacts, etc.)	Approximate Value

USEFUL TENANT TIPS

Entertainment Equipment	
Item Description (TV, stereo, speakers, recording devices, etc.)	

Furniture	
Item Description	Approximate Value

Kitchen Utensils	
Item Description (silverware, pots, pans, dishes, cups, etc.)	Approximate Value

PERSONAL INVENTORY LIST

Jewelry

Item Description	Approximate Value

Art/Pictures/Paintings

Item Description	Approximate Value

Tools

Item Description (hand, power)	Approximate Value

Vehicles

Item Description (cars, trucks, motorcycles)	Approximate Value

Weapons

Item Description	Approximate Value

Miscellaneous

Item Description	Approximate Value

ACKNOWLEDGMENTS

I WOULD LIKE TO ACKNOWLEDGE Lena and Barry Prentice for their training, guidance, and support over the years as I was developing my career as a home inspector. Without them, my path in life would have been much different, and not as much fun or rewarding.

Thank you.

UPCOMING TITLES

- *Useful Homeowner Tips*

- *Useful Home Buying Tips*
  (coming in 2025)

- *Useful Home Selling Tips*
  (coming in 2025)

- *Useful Residential Home Landlord Tips*
  (coming in 2026)

- *Useful Manufactured Housing Ownership Tips*
  (coming in 2026)

- *Useful New Build Ownership Tips*
  (coming in 2026)

- *What You Need to Know About Fix-n-Flip Properties*
  (coming in 2026)

ABOUT THE AUTHOR

JIM CAMP was born and raised in Denver, Colorado. His interests were anything mechanical, and he enjoyed tearing things apart and putting them back together again: everything from lawn mowers to motorcycles and automobile engines. After he graduated from high school, he joined the navy during the Vietnam Era. When he returned, he went to night school and obtained his BS degree in mechanical engineering. He had several jobs as a physical science technician, quality engineer, project engineer and quality/test engineer before leaving corporate America.

In December of 1993, Jim decided to start his own business and founded Metropolitan Home Inspections. He soon realized that although challenging, it was also very rewarding, as he was helping people understand the overall condition of the home or rental property they were about to choose.

He is a certified home inspector through the American Society of Home Inspectors (ASHI) and is also licensed with the State of Colorado, Department of Regulatory Agencies (DORA), and certified through the National Radon Proficiency Program (NRPP) to perform Radon testing throughout the State.

He has inspected thousands of single-family homes, up to sixteen-unit multifamily complexes, townhomes, condominiums, manufactured homes, cabins, and small commercial buildings. Many of these inspections were rentals or rentals with an option to buy. This is where he honed his skills and what prompted him to write this book, which was solely based upon his experiences, along with viewing the conditions of many of the properties he's inspected throughout the years.

Jim takes pride in what he does and thoroughly explains to each tenant the workings and overall condition of the home, regardless of what type of structure it is.

www.ingramcontent.com/pod-product-compliance
Lightning Source LLC
Chambersburg PA
CBHW020557030426
42337CB00013B/1123